MW00878172

VOLODYMYR
ZELENSKY

VOLODYMYR ZELENSKY

Heroic Leader of Ukraine

MARI BOLTE

LERNER PUBLICATIONS ◆ MINNEAPOLIS

Lerner Publications Company
An imprint of Lerner Publishing Group, Inc.
241 First Avenue North
Minneapolis, MN 55401 USA

For reading levels and more information, look up this title at www.lernerbooks.com.

Main body text set in Rotis Serif Std.
Typeface provided by Monotype.

The images in this book are used with the permission of: Sean Gallup/Staff/Getty Images, p.2; Igor Golovniov/ZUMAPRESS/Newscom, p.6; Brendan Hoffman/Stringer/Getty Images, p.8; Andrew J.Kurbiko/Wikimedia, p.10; Everett Collection/Shutterstock, p.11; Cryptic-waveform/ Wikimedia, p.12; Astel7/Wikimedia, p.13; Review News/Shutterstock, p.14; Vadim Chuprina/ Wikimedia, p.15; Review News/Shutterstock, p.16; WPA Pool/Getty Images, p.17; Christian Marquardt/Stringer/Getty Images, p.18; Alexey Lesik/Shutterstock, p.19; Dmytro Larin/ Shutterstock, p.21; Brendan Hoffman/Stringer/Getty Images, p.22; Brendan Hoffman/Stringer/ Getty Images, p.23; Brendan Hoffman/Stringer/Getty Images, p.24; Sean Gallup/Staff/Getty Images, p.26; Pool/Getty Images, p.27; Pool/Getty Images, 28; Pyotr Sivkov/TASS/Sipa USA/ Newscom, p.30; Omar Marques/Stringer/Getty Images, p.31; Sea Salt/Shutterstock, p.32; Nick. mon/Wikimedia, p.33; Chris McGrath/Staff/Getty Images, p.34; Igor Golovniov/ZUMAPRESS/ Newscom, p.36; Sorbis/Shutterstock, p.37; Pool/Getty Images, p.38

Front cover: © Anadolu Agency/Contributor/Getty Images

Library of Congress Cataloging-in-Publication Data

Names: Bolte, Mari, author.
Title: Volodymyr Zelensky : heroic leader of Ukraine / Mari Bolte.
Other titles: Heroic leader of Ukraine
Description: Minneapolis : Lerner Publications, [2023] | Series: Gateway biographies | Includes
   bibliographical references and index. | Audience: Ages 9–14 | Audience: Grades 4–6 |
   Summary: "Zelensky got his start as an actor, running for president of Ukraine as a populist
   candidate in 2019. He seemed an unlikely hero, yet he quickly revealed his resolve as Putin's
   forces threatened his homeland"– Provided by publisher.
Identifiers: LCCN 2022018565 (print) | LCCN 2022018566 (ebook) | ISBN 9781728487830
   (library binding) | ISBN 9781728487847 (paperback) | ISBN 9781728487854 (ebook)
Subjects: LCSH: Zelensky, Volodymyr, 1978-–Juvenile literature. | Presidents–Ukraine–
   Biography–Juvenile literature. | Actors–Ukraine–Biography–Juvenile literature. |
   Ukraine–Politics and government–21st century–Juvenile literature. | Ukraine–Foreign
   relations–Russia (Federation)–Juvenile literature. | Russia (Federation)–Foreign relations–
   Ukraine–Juvenile literature.
Classification: LCC DK508.851.Z45 B65 2023 (print) | LCC DK508.851.Z45 (ebook) | DDC
   947.7086092 [B]–dc23/eng/20220429

LC record available at https://lccn.loc.gov/2022018565
LC ebook record available at https://lccn.loc.gov/2022018566

Manufactured in the United States of America
1-52929-51010-5/3/2022

TABLE OF CONTENTS

Ukraine president Volodymyr Zelensky speaks to his country's citizens on February 24, 2022.

Early on February 24, 2022, the people of Ukraine woke to the sound of explosions. Russia had begun what it called "special military operations." Nearly two hundred thousand Russian troops spilled across the border between the two countries. Planes flew overhead. Russia launched missiles. It attacked major Ukrainian cities, including the capital city of Kyiv. Air raid sirens blared. The Ukrainians wondered what would come next.

Later that morning, President Volodymyr Zelensky appeared on TVs across Ukraine. He said that he had called the president of Russia, Vladimir Putin. Putin had not answered. Zelensky spoke to the people of both Russia and Ukraine and told them that the Russian attack was a big step toward war. He issued a warning: "If we'll be attacked by the [enemy] troops, if they try to take our country away from us, our freedom, our lives, the lives of our children, we will defend ourselves. Not attack, but defend ourselves. And when you will be attacking us, you will see our faces, not our backs, but our faces."

Zelensky celebrates his presidential victory in April 2019.

Zelensky had been elected president nearly three years before the attack, on April 21, 2019. A former comedian and movie star, he was not a traditional politician. He had run for office because he was tired of government corruption. He knew Ukraine was tired of leaders who wanted unquestioning loyalty from Ukraine's people. He told voters he would bring a new wave of moral leaders. His message spoke to the people, and he won his election easily.

Since Zelensky's swearing-in on May 20, 2019, some people had started to doubt his leadership. But then Russia attacked. Suddenly, one of the biggest crises of the 21st century had begun. And Zelensky rose to the challenge.

ABOUT UKRAINE

Ukraine is in eastern Europe. It is the second-largest country there, after its neighbor to the east, Russia. In Ukraine's north is its capital, Kyiv. In the south is the Black Sea. More than forty-four million people call Ukraine home.

The country is full of natural resources. It has the second-largest natural gas reserves in Europe. Large stores of iron, coal, lithium, and uranium are important to manufacturing products around the world, such as airplanes, engines, and batteries. Thanks to its rich soil, good for growing grains such as wheat and corn, Ukraine is known as "Europe's breadbasket."

Many countries have fought to control Ukraine, including Poland, Czechoslovakia, Romania, and Russia. Some of those countries have come and gone. Czechoslovakia, for example, split into two countries in 1993—the Czech Republic and Slovakia. Others, such as Romania, have gained or lost parts of their own territories. Some conflicts go back centuries.

Ukraine was part of a country called the Soviet Union (USSR) for seventy years before becoming an independent nation in 1991 after the USSR dissolved. Gaining independence doesn't mean interest in Ukraine has waned, though. Russia, the dominant republic of the former USSR, has been trying to retake Ukraine ever since.

Ukraine is not part of the European Union (EU) or the North Atlantic Treaty Organization (NATO). But it does receive financial, humanitarian, and military support from the EU, NATO, and the United States.

Present-day Kryvyi Rih, Ukraine, Zelensky's birthplace

BORN IN THE USSR

Volodymyr Zelensky was born on January 25, 1978, in Kryvyi Rih, Ukraine, then part of the USSR. His parents, Oleksander and Rimma, are of Jewish descent. Jewish people, or Jews, are an ethnic and religious group. They have been persecuted for thousands of years. Zelensky's grandfather Semyon fought in the Soviet army against Nazi Germany during World War II (1939–1945). Some of his extended family members died in the Holocaust at the hands of the Nazis, along with one million other Ukrainian Jews.

Zelensky is proud of his grandfather. In 2020 he said, "He survived World War II contributing to the victory over Nazism and hateful ideology. Two years after the war, his son was born. And his grandson was born thirty-one years after. Forty years later, his grandson became president. And today he stands before you."

Being Jewish in Ukraine was not easy during Zelensky's childhood. His family lived in the only Soviet area where Jews were allowed to live. It was called the Pale of Settlement. Russia had forbidden Jews from living anywhere else since the 1700s. Even the people who lived in the settlement were not safe from harassment and terror. Practicing Judaism was not allowed, though some people did it in secret.

In the early 1900s, about five million Jews lived in the Pale of Settlement.

WHAT WAS THE USSR?

The United Socialist Soviet Republic, also called the USSR and the Soviet Union, was formed in 1922. It was made up of fifteen Soviet republics, including Russia and Ukraine. At its height, it was one of the biggest and most powerful nations in the world. The USSR was a Communist country. Communists believe that all property, including land and personal property, should not be owned by individuals. Everyone works together, and everyone gets paid as much as they need and no more.

The practice of Communism did not work well in the USSR. There was a lot of confusion and disorganization that led to starvation. People began to resist—especially people in Ukraine. To keep Ukrainians in line, entire towns were cut off from food, and people were forbidden to leave to find any. From 1931 to 1934, about four million Ukrainians died from starvation. The famine was called Holodomor, a combination of the Ukrainian words holod (hunger) and mor (extermination).

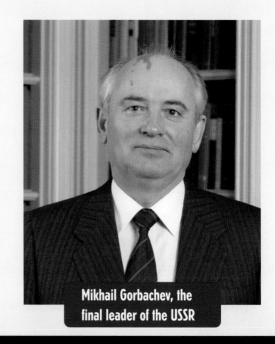

Mikhail Gorbachev, the final leader of the USSR

The USSR fell apart in 1991. The republics began breaking free. On August 24, 1991, Ukraine declared its independence. It was the end of the USSR.

Kyiv National Economic University is Ukraine's top-rated economics school.

The Zelensky family spoke Russian at home, but Volodymyr also learned Ukrainian and English. When he was very young, the family moved to Erdenet, Mongolia, where Oleksander had taken a job. Oleksander was a mathematician and scientist. Rimma was a civil engineer. The family later returned to Kryvyi Rih so Volodymyr could start primary school.

Volodymyr was a good student. At sixteen, he scored so high on an international English exam that he could have studied abroad in Israel. Although the education would have been free, his father wouldn't let him go. Instead, Volodymyr went to the Kyiv National Economic University in 1995. In 2000 he graduated with a law degree. But he didn't want to practice law. He wanted to be an entertainer.

PUT ON A SHOW

Zelensky had always liked to perform. He had been part of plays, musicals, and comedy productions in the past. He set his sights on *KVN* (Klub vesyólykh i nakhódchivykh, or the Club of the Funny and Inventive People). *KVN* is a popular and long-running TV show in Ukraine. People have watched it since 1961.

Inspired by the show, local *KVN* competitions are held throughout the former Soviet Union. They range from small leagues of just a few casual teams to the major leagues of professional comedians. More than forty thousand people participate on three thousand teams in more than one hundred cities.

Zelensky (*center*) and his group, Kvartal 95, were a strong comedic force.

Teams compete in a series of humorous games of improv and sketch comedy. Improv challenges comedians to make up jokes on the spot. Sketch comedy involves short scenes performed by a group. The jokes and sketches are judged by guests. The highest-rated leagues, the Highest and the Premier, are broadcast on TV and judged by celebrities.

In 1997 Zelensky joined a team of other Ukrainians to compete in the *KVN* Major League. They won. The group called themselves Kvartal 95. The name comes from a famous road crossing in Kryvyi Rih and means "Quarter 95." Soon Kvartal 95 began appearing on the actual *KVN* show. They were competitors until 2003.

Zelensky helped create Studio Kvartal 95, one of Ukraine's most successful entertainment studios.

BE CREATIVE

In 2003 Kvartal 95 started writing and producing its own TV shows for the channel 1+1. Their projects included TV shows, movies, cartoons, festivals, and concerts. Zelensky wrote and performed the kinds of projects he liked best.

Zelensky said, "Our ambitious objective is to make the world a better place, a kinder and more joyful place with the help of those tools that we have; that is humor and creativity. We are moving towards this goal, trying to conquer the whole world, of course [wink emoticon]."

The studio also took on social projects to support people in need, especially children and young people. Members from the group visited students who were interested in learning about video creation. They also took interest in the Kyiv Boarding School No. 15. Students attend the boarding school while recovering from medical procedures for polio and cerebral palsy. Kvartal 95 brought gifts, visited, and played football. They donated movie tickets too.

The year 2003 was also important for Zelensky's personal life. On September 6, he married Olena Kiyashko. They had known each other since childhood, though they weren't friends. They met again as college students. Olena studied architecture at the Faculty of Civil Engineering. She and Zelensky both liked to write, and they produced scripts and screenplays together. Olena was already involved in several TV projects when they married. Their first child, Oleksandra, was born in 2004. Kyrylo, their son, was born in 2013.

Zelensky and his wife, Olena

Tantsi z zirkamy, Ukraine's version of *Dancing with the Stars*, began in 2006. Zelensky was part of that first season. He danced wearing a pink jumpsuit, tangoed, and even did choreography while blindfolded. He and his partner, Ukrainian dancer Olena Shoptenko, won the competition.

In 2008 he began acting in movies. The following year, he starred in *No Love in the City*, a movie he also cowrote. He played a dentist with an interesting dating life. Two sequels were made in 2010 and 2012.

Zelensky was the voice of the children's book character Paddington Bear in two live-action animated films.

With Studio Kvartal 95, Zelensky balanced humor with social responsibility.

Rzhevskiy Versus Napoleon (2012) was a historical comedy. Zelensky was cast as Napoleon Bonaparte during the invasion of Russia. *8 First Dates* (2012) and *8 New Dates* (2015) were romantic comedies. He voiced Paddington Bear in the Ukrainian version of *Paddington* and *Paddington 2* in 2014 and 2017. Zelensky later said, "In my previous profession . . . I wanted to get [an] Oscar. I wanted to be very popular in the USA."

Zelensky served as Studio Kvartal 95's creative director and executive producer until 2011. He balanced the job with his acting career. Then he was promoted to an executive position with the channel InterTV. But in 2013, he returned to Studio Kvartal 95.

SERVANT OF THE PEOPLE

In 2015 Zelensky landed the starring role of Vasily Petrovich Goloborodko in the TV show *Servant of the People.* His character was a high school history teacher. One day Goloborodko rants about the government. The government is corrupt, he says. Officials are too busy making themselves rich to care about regular people. One of his students posts the speech, and it goes viral on social media. People crowdfund Goloborodko's candidacy, and his name appears on the ballot. To everyone's surprise, Goloborodko ends up being elected president. Although the story was made up, real Ukrainian problems were addressed on the show. A major theme was that Goloborodko was often in over his head but willing to try.

Kvartal 95 created a political party based off the show in March 2018. And on the last day of that year, Zelensky announced his candidacy for president. He ran under the Servant of the People Party. The final episodes of the TV show aired during the presidential campaign.

"People want to see a president . . . with the same moral values. They're fed up with the establishment. People want something new," Zelensky said.

Some people have compared Zelensky's TV work with UK prime minister Boris Johnson's appearances on *Have I Got News for You* or former US president Donald Trump on *The Apprentice.* But others have pointed out that *Servant of the People* serves as Zelensky's origin story. It gives viewers a glimpse into who the future president will become.

UKRAINIAN POLITICS

In Ukraine the president is elected by popular vote. They serve five-year terms. The prime minister is appointed by the president and other lawmakers. Then the president and prime minister choose members of the cabinet. The cabinet members oversee day-to-day operations.

Ukraine is a unitary republic. The president has top authority. Great Britain is another example of a unitary state. Since its independence in 1991, Ukraine has elected six presidents.

Leonid Kravchuk, the first president of Ukraine

WINNING THE PEOPLE

Unlike some traditional politicians, Zelensky did not do a lot of in-person campaigning. He let his Goloborodko character speak for him. He also used social media. His voters found him on YouTube, Instagram, and Facebook. He posted workout videos, pictures of his dogs, and outdoor selfies. Funny sketches and short speeches were common too. The strategy worked.

Zelensky used selfies to connect with fans and voters.

There were two rounds of elections. During the first round, voters had thirty-nine candidates to choose from. More than 4.5 million people cast their ballot for Zelensky. He got more votes than the second- and third-place candidates combined. "No Joke: Ukraine TV Comedian Wins Election's First Round," *The New York Times* quipped. Although his opponent mocked him and accused him of being a weak president who would fold under pressure from Vladimir Putin, Zelensky took it seriously. He said, "I want to thank all Ukrainians who voted today not just for kicks. This is only the first step toward a great victory."

Zelensky ran on the message of unity. He wanted to celebrate people's differences but also to embrace Ukrainian independence. Two weeks before the second-round vote, he said, "They divided us . . . but we are all Ukrainians . . . In the north, south, east, west and center . . . Ukrainian and Russian speakers . . . We are different, but so similar. We are uniting to move forward."

Then Ukraine president Petro Poroshenko (*left*) and Zelensky meet for a debate in early 2019.

Zelensky casts his vote in the 2019 Ukrainian presidential election.

During the second round of elections, Zelensky earned 73 percent of the vote. On April 22, 2019, he was named the victor. He was the youngest president, with the youngest spouse, in Ukraine's history. Ukraine also became the only country outside Israel with a president and prime minister who were Jewish.

Some people were skeptical. "He can't imagine how hard this system is to break," said a Ukrainian political analyst. "He probably thinks like a film director . . . and real life is much more complicated."

Petro Poroshenko, the previous president and second-place finisher, said, "I would like to remind everyone that this is not a joke. This is the election of the commander in chief."

Zelensky wanted to prove he was serious about the job. During his first official speech, he spoke to lawmakers by saying, "I do not want my picture in your offices: The President is not an icon, an idol, or a portrait. Hang your kids' photos instead and look at them each time you are making a decision." He also said, "Every one of us bears responsibility for Ukraine, which we will leave to our children. . . . We have to be united, and only then are we strong."

Zelensky addresses questions about Hunter Biden in fall 2019.

MR. PRESIDENT

Zelensky was thrust onto the world stage after phone calls from then US president Donald Trump in July 2019. Trump asked Zelensky to investigate Trump's rival for the upcoming 2020 election, Joe Biden. Trump also requested information on Biden's son Hunter. Trump believed there was a computer server in Ukraine with the information, and he wanted Zelensky to find it.

Trump had recently blocked $400 million of military aid to Ukraine. He told Zelensky that the aid would be released if Zelensky helped him. Zelensky was also supposed to publicly announce that the investigations were taking place.

This was illegal. The US House of Representatives investigated. Ukraine's aid was sent in September. Then the House moved to impeach President Trump.

IMPEACHMENT

Donald Trump was the third US president to be impeached. He was the only one to be impeached twice. The US Constitution states that the president, vice president, and civil officers can be impeached for "Treason, Bribery, or other high Crimes and Misdemeanors." The House of Representatives impeaches a president, and then the Senate holds a trial. If the president is convicted, they are removed from office. Both times Trump was impeached, he was acquitted. This means he was allowed to stay in office.

The delayed aid from the United States was intended to train special forces and provide soldiers with new weapons. Ukraine had been a site of conflict since 2014, in the regions of Donbas and Crimea.

One of Zelensky's election promises was peace in Donbas. In 2014 rebel soldiers supported by the Russian government entered the Donbas region in southeast Ukraine. Fighting broke out. The rebels took control and declared the area a republic. They also moved to occupy Crimea.

More than fourteen thousand people have been killed since the Donbas conflict began. Putin has justified his support of the rebels by claiming genocide against Russian speakers has taken place there. Genocide is the intentional act of destroying a group of people. However, many people point out that Zelensky himself speaks Russian.

In 2019 Zelensky and Putin met for the first time. A cease-fire was agreed upon, and prisoner exchanges were planned. Critics thought Zelensky was too timid. By 2021 fighting resumed, and Russian soldiers were moving closer to the Ukrainian border.

The first meeting between Zelensky (*left*) and Russian president Vladimir Putin (*center right*)

THE CRIMEAN CONFLICT

Crimea is a peninsula in southern Ukraine. It is nearly surrounded by water. A thin strip of land connects it to Ukraine. It's an important location for trade and control of the region. People have fought over Crimea for hundreds of years. In 1991 it became a self-governing part of Ukraine. Russia and Ukraine shared a military port in Crimea on the Black Sea. Having aircraft carriers there allowed Russia to send jets deeper into Europe.

In late 2013, Viktor Yanukovych, then president of Ukraine, met with the EU. The EU offered to lend Ukraine money and open its borders for trading. Initially, Yanukovych said he would sign. Then he refused altogether. Thousands of people protested on the streets of Kyiv. Yanukovych fled the country in February 2014.

Soon after he left, armed men entered Crimea. By March they controlled the whole peninsula. They wore Russian uniforms, carried Russian guns, and drove Russian vehicles. Putin said they were local men who had formed self-defense groups. Later, though, he would admit they were Russian troops.

On March 16, government officials in Crimea held a vote. They had two choices—join with Russia or become independent. There was no third option to reunite with Ukraine. Many pro-Ukraine officials were not at the vote. No international witnesses were there either. Putin declared a nearly unanimous vote to join Russia had taken place. On March 21, Russia took full control of Crimea.

In 2020 the COVID-19 pandemic swept across the globe. The ongoing conflict with Russia made it difficult to get resources to Ukraine. In addition to the pandemic, many Ukrainians faced safety concerns from war and had to flee areas of danger. War-related injuries were more pressing to health-care workers than giving out vaccines.

Zelensky's response to the pandemic, in the face of war dangers, was swift. He banned mass events. Schools and transportation systems were off limits. Restaurants shut down.

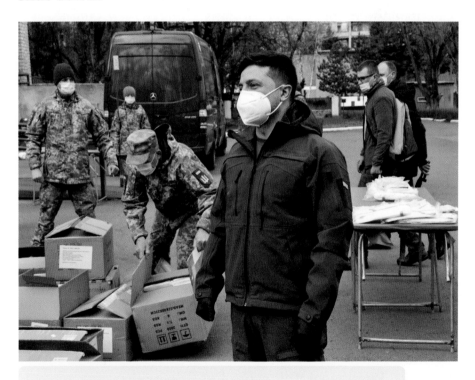

From the start of the COVID-19 pandemic, Zelensky showed his support for health-care workers.

Ukrainians displaced by the war also had to contend with a pandemic.

The virus took its toll on Ukraine. The economy was already weak because of the fighting, and nearly five hundred thousand people lost their jobs. Vaccination rollouts were slow too. By November only one in five people had gotten vaccinated. In November Zelensky tested positive for COVID-19 and was hospitalized for a few days. But he continued to work. And in March 2021, he posted a photo on social media. It showed him receiving his vaccine on the frontline. "There is nothing to be afraid of. I am setting a personal example," the caption said.

NATO Headquarters, Brussels, Belgium

THE FIGHT IS HERE

For many years, Ukraine has asked to be part of NATO. NATO was founded after World War II. Its goal was to provide countries peace and security against the USSR. It also promotes the spread of democracy. NATO is currently made up of thirty members, including the United States and European countries such as Germany, France, and the United Kingdom.

Membership means fellow NATO countries provide defensive and offensive military support when needed. Allowing Ukraine to join would obligate NATO to defend Ukraine from possible Russian attacks.

A new country must be invited to join by an existing NATO member. And the vote for membership must be unanimous. Ukraine has not yet been invited. However, the United States has hinted that Ukraine would be part of NATO since 2008. This mixed message put Ukraine in a tricky position. It was well known that Putin wanted to control Ukraine, but nobody knew who would step up to stop him.

In early 2021, Russian troops began gathering near the Ukraine border. By November satellite images showed around one hundred thousand troops ready to invade. Putin called for NATO troops and weapons to pull back. And he demanded Ukraine be barred from joining NATO.

WHO IS VLADIMIR PUTIN?

Russian president Vladimir Putin first served from 1999 to 2008. Then he was the prime minister until 2012, before resuming the role of president. He is also a former officer of the KGB, the Soviet Union's intelligence agency. Putin is an autocrat. That means he has absolute power over Russia. He wants to control every country once under Soviet power. He also wants to turn away from the western world.

THE INVASION BEGINS

People in Russia were told that their troops were part of a "special military operation." The soldiers would play a role in freeing Ukraine from fascism. Fascism is a political ideology in which leaders forcefully stop any kind of opposition to their power. But on February 17, 2022, Zelensky reported that pro-Russian forces had attacked a civilian area. A kindergarten was damaged. Another twenty-two areas in Donbas had been attacked. Putin urged Ukrainian soldiers to surrender, and he warned other countries not to interfere. The cease-fire was over.

Territorial defense units serve as backup for Ukraine's armed forces to protect the country.

Zelensky responded by addressing Russian citizens on February 23. "You have been told that this flame will bring liberation to Ukraine's people," he said. "But the Ukrainian people are free. They remember their own past and will build their own future."

The Russian invasion began on February 24. Zelensky was at home. At 4:50 a.m., his family woke him, saying that there had been explosions. He called a state of emergency. The cities of Kyiv, Kherson, and Mariupol were bombed. Some people there lost electricity. They didn't have food or water. Medical supplies were scarce. Attempts to evacuate citizens were unsuccessful. Bridges and roads were destroyed. But the people were also united. "On the first day of the war it became clear there was no panic," First Lady Olena Zelenska said. "When the attack took place, we did not become a 'frightened crowd,' as the enemy had hoped. No. We became an organized community. . . . Everyone came together to protect their home."

And protect their home they did. Defenders shot down Russian jets and attacked Russian soldiers and tanks. They made homemade explosives. Food and water supplies were distributed, and money was sent to Ukraine's army and civilian fighters. Tens of thousands of people showed up to fight for their country. And they followed the example set online by their president. Videos, livestreams, and TikToks from inside Ukraine flooded the internet.

On February 26, the United States offered to help Zelensky evacuate the country. It was reported that he replied, "The fight is here; I need ammunition, not a ride."

HE DIDN'T CHOOSE TO FIGHT

On February 24, leaders of the EU gathered to discuss putting sanctions on Russia. Some leaders were reluctant. The sanctions were harsh and would be added to sanctions that were already in place.

During the meeting, Zelensky video called from a battlefield in Kyiv. He pled with the leaders. He asked them to allow Ukraine into the EU. He said his people needed help. It was an emotional call, and it ended when he told them that may be the last time they saw him alive. Soon after that call, new sanctions were put on Russia.

Zelensky appeals to Ukraine's western neighbors for support in February 2022.

A Ukrainian political analyst said that Zelensky "didn't choose to fight, and he is not a president of a wartime. But since yesterday, when it became clear from his intelligence what shape the attack would take, he is acting exactly how a president should act in the wartime regime."

SANCTIONS

Sanctions are penalties placed on a country. They are meant to prevent that country from acting aggressively. For example, one sanction placed on Russia prevented factories from getting parts they needed to make vehicles, especially tanks. Russian planes were not allowed to land in the United States, United Kingdom, EU, or Canada. Money and properties in those countries that belonged to rich Russians were frozen—and that included billions of dollars belonging to Russia's main bank. Money transfers could no longer be made to Russia, and the world would no longer be buying Russian oil and gas. Many major companies stopped operating in Russia too, including Starbucks, McDonald's, and Coca-Cola.

On March 5, Zelensky had a video meeting with more than three hundred members of the US Congress. He asked for more military aid and a no-fly zone over Ukraine. No-fly zones are areas where military action is taken against unlawful aircraft. He also asked for planes for his own pilots. Between August 2021 and April 2022, the United States sent more than $3 billion in aid to Ukraine.

During the call with Congress, two senators shared screenshots of Zelensky. The move put his secret location at risk. People around the world worried for his safety. That same day, Netflix resumed streaming *Servant of the People.* Zelensky's face was everywhere.

The US Congress listens to Zelensky's requests for assistance in March 2022.

Zelensky knew he might be alone in the fight, and he knew he had a target on his back. "The enemy has marked me as enemy number one," he said. For a few days, his location was kept secret. The rest of the Zelensky family was in hiding. But Zelensky himself didn't go into hiding. On March 7, he shared a video from the president's desk in Kyiv. He said, "I'm not hiding. And I'm not afraid of anyone."

By April 6, Russian forces had withdrawn from Kyiv. They turned their focus to eastern Ukraine. But the danger wasn't over. They left live mines behind. Experts believed that once troops regrouped in Donbas, the Russians would return.

On April 14, Ukrainian troops attacked the Russian cruiser Moskva. The 600-foot (183-m) warship sank in the Black Sea. Moskva was the flagship of Russia's Black Sea fleet. While not a huge military loss, it demonstrated weaknesses in the Russian naval command.

When asked what a Ukrainian victory looks like, Zelensky once said, "Victory is being able to save as many lives as possible. . . . I don't know how long the war will last, but we will fight to the last city we have."

Zelensky's future is unknown. His advisors have told reporters that they believe he is ready to die for his cause. He does not have years of training as a politician or in military strategy. He was a comedian. But Hollywood producers are already talking about a biopic about his life and the war. To this Zelensky said, "It's very serious, it's not a movie . . . I'm not iconic, I think Ukraine is iconic."

IMPORTANT DATES

January 25, 1978 Volodymyr Zelensky is born in Kryvyi Rih, Ukraine.

August 24, 1991 Ukraine declares its independence from the USSR.

1995 Zelensky starts classes at Kyiv National Economic University.

1997 Zelensky joins with a team of Ukrainians to compete in the *KVN* Major League. They win the competition and form Kvartal 95.

2000 Zelensky graduates with a law degree.

2003 Kvartal 95 starts writing and producing its own shows.

September 6, 2003 Zelensky marries Olena Kiyashko.

2004 Oleksandra is born.

2006 Zelensky and his partner, Olena Shoptenko, win the first season of Ukraine's *Dancing with the Stars*.

2008 Zelensky begins acting in movies.

2009 Zelensky cowrites and stars in *No Love in the City*.

2011 InterTV hires Zelensky to an executive position.

2013 Kyrylo is born.

2014 The Ukrainian version of *Paddington* is released, with Zelensky voicing the title character.

2014 Rebel soldiers enter Donbas and Crimea.

2015 The first season of *Servant of the People* comes out, with Zelensky in the starring role. The show runs through 2019.

2018 Kvartal 95 creates the Servant of the People Party.

December 31, 2018 Zelensky announces his run for the presidency.

March 31, 2019 The first round of elections takes place. Zelensky receives more votes than the second- and third-place candidates combined.

April 21, 2019 The second round of elections takes place.

April 22, 2019 Zelensky is elected president.

May 20, 2019 Zelensky is sworn in as president.

July 2019 Telephone calls with US president Donald Trump bring attention to Ukraine. Trump is later impeached for his illegal actions.

December 9, 2019 Zelensky meets with Vladimir Putin for the first time.

February 17, 2022 Pro-Russian forces attack a civilian area in Ukraine, damaging a kindergarten.

February 23, 2022 Zelensky addresses Russian citizens, asking them not to support war.

February 24, 2022 Russia invades Ukraine.

February 24, 2022 European leaders gather to discuss sanctioning Russia.

SOURCE NOTES

7   "Russia-Ukraine Crisis: Zelenskyy's Address in Full," *Al Jazeera*, February 24, 2022, https://www.aljazeera.com /news/2022/2/24/russia-ukraine-crisis-president-zelenskky -speech-in-full.

10   "Volodymyr Zelenskyy Told the Story of His Family During a Joint Speech with Prime Minister Benjamin Netanyahu," The Presidential Office of Ukraine, February 24, 2022, https://web.archive.org/web/20220225123949/https://www .president.gov.ua/en/news/volodimir-zelenskij-rozpoviv -istoriyu-svoyeyi-rodini-pid-cha-59437.

16   "About," Kvartal 95, https://kvartal95.com/en/about/.

19   Christiane Amanpour, Twitter, February 17, 2020, https ://twitter.com/amanpour/status/1229473275442614277.

20   Bryan Pietsch and Sammy Westfall, "What to Know about Volodymyr Zelensky, Ukraine's TV President Turned Wartime Leader," *The Washington Post*, March 1, 2022, https://www.washingtonpost.com/world/2022/03/01 /ukraine-president-volodymyr-zelensky-russia/.

23   Iuliia Mendel and Neil MacFarquhar, "No Joke: Ukraine TV Comedian Wins Election's First Round," *The New York Times*, March 31, 2019, https://www.nytimes .com/2019/03/31/world/europe/ukraine-election-comedian .html.

23   Nina Jankowicz, "This Ukrainian Presidential Candidate Is Challenging Language Divisions with a Message of Unity," *The World: Global Politics*, April 19, 2019, https://theworld .org/stories/2019-04-19/ukrainian-presidential-candidate -challenging-language-divisions-message-unity.

25   David L. Stern and Anton Troianovski, "Comedian Who Plays the President on TV on Track for Big First-Round Win in (Real) Ukrainian Presidential Election," *The Washington Post*, April 1, 2019, https://www .washingtonpost.com/world/comedian-on-track-for -big-first-round-win-ukrainian-presidential-election -results-show/2019/04/01/5265eac2-5249-11e9-bdb7 -44f948cc0605_story.html.

25   Stern.

25   Heather Wake, "Zelenskyy's 2019 Inaugural Speech Goes Viral for Its Exemplary Display of Humanity in Leadership," *Upworthy*, March 1, 2022, https://www .upworthy.com/zelenskyy-speech-inauguration.

27   "The United States Constitution, Article II, Section 4," April 15, 2022, https://constitution.congress.gov/browse/essay /artII-S4-1-1/ALDE_00000282/.

31   Zelensky official, Instagram, March 2, 2022, https://www .instagram.com/p/CL6efNOFZgN/.

35   "Ukraine Conflict: What We Know about the Invasion,"
      BBC, February 24, 2022, https://www.bbc.com/news/world
      -europe-60504334.

35   "Ukraine's First Lady Says Her Kids Haven't Seen Their Dad
      in Weeks but Look Out for Each Other," *People*, April 13,
      2022, https://people.com/politics/ukraine-first-lady-kids
      -havent-seen-dad-month-look-out-for-each-other/.

35   Embassy of Ukraine to the UK, Twitter, February 26, 2022,
      https://twitter.com/UkrEmbLondon/status
      /1497506134692970499.

37   Valerie Hopkins, "Zelensky Steps into a Role Few Expected:
      Ukraine's Wartime President," *The New York Times*,
      February 24, 2022, https://www.nytimes.com/2022/02/24
      /world/europe/ukraine-zelensky-speech.html.

39   "Zelensky Says He Is 'Enemy Number One,'" *The Wall
      Street Journal*, February 25, 2022, https://www.wsj.com
      /livecoverage/russia-ukraine-latest-news/card/zelensky
      -says-he-is-enemy-number-one--
      sEGkX3kCrJKHQhcL3MH4.

39   Shawna Chen, "I'm Not Hiding. And I'm Not Afraid of
      Anyone," *Yahoo*, March 7, 2022, https://www.yahoo.com
      /entertainment/m-not-hiding-im-not-013635820.html.

39   "Volodymyr Zelensky in His Own Words," *The Economist*,
      March 27, 2022, https://www.economist.com
      /europe/2022/03/27/volodymyr-zelensky-in-his-own
      -words.

39 Philissa Cramer/JTA, "18 Things to Know about Volodymyr Zelensky, 'Paddington' Voice and Jewish Defender of Ukraine," *The Jerusalem Post*, March 2, 2022, https://www .jpost.com/j-spot/article-699073.

SELECTED BIBLIOGRAPHY

Al Jazeera Staff. "Who Is Volodymyr Zelenskyy, Europe's Most Vulnerable President?" *Al Jazeera*, February 25, 2022. https ://www.aljazeera.com/news/2022/2/25/who-is-volodymyr -zelenskyy-europes-most-vulnerable-president.

"Conflict in Ukraine." Global Conflict Tracker, Council on Foreign Relations, March 29, 2022. https://www.cfr.org/global-conflict -tracker/conflict/conflict-ukraine.

Fitzgerald, Madeline. "Russia Invades Ukraine: A Timeline of the Crisis." *US News*, February 22, 2022. https://www.usnews .com/news/best-countries/slideshows/a-timeline-of-the-russia -ukraine-conflict.

Kirby, Jen, and Jonathan Guyer. "Russia's War in Ukraine Explained." *Vox*, March 6, 2022. https://www.vox.com/2022 /2/23/22948534/russia-ukraine-war-putin-explosions -invasion-explained.

Peitsch, Bryan, and Sammy Westfall. "What to Know about Volodymyr Zelensky, Ukraine's TV President Turned Wartime Leader." *The Washington Post*, March 2, 2022. https://www .washingtonpost.com/world/2022/03/01/ukraine-president -volodymyr-zelensky-russia/.

"Russia-Ukraine Crisis: Zelenskyy's Address in Full." *Al Jazeera*, February 24, 2022. https://www.aljazeera.com/news/2022/2/24 /russia-ukraine-crisis-president-zelenskky-speech-in-full.

"Volodymyr Zelensky in His Own Words." *The Economist*, March 27, 2022. https://www.economist.com/europe/2022/03/27 /volodymyr-zelensky-in-his-own-words.

FURTHER READING

BOOKS

Britton, Tamara L. *War in Ukraine.* Minneapolis, MN: ABDO, 2022.

Klepeis, Alicia. *Ukraine.* Minneapolis, MN: Bellwether Media, 2021.

Roland, James. *Impeachment: Donald Trump and the History of Presidents in Peril.* Minneapolis, MN: Lerner Publications, 2021.

WEBSITES

Britannica Kids: Volodymyr Zelensky
https://kids.britannica.com/kids/article/Volodymyr
-Zelensky/634177

How To . . . Show Your Support for Peace
http://cdn.subscriptions.dennis.co.uk/sites/default/files/2022
-03/99_Peace.pdf

Time for Kids: War in Ukraine
https://www.timeforkids.com/g56/war-in-ukraine-2/?rl=en-880

INDEX